ANIMAL IDIOMS

Stubborn as a Mule: Are Mules Headstrong?

BY MATT LILLEY

CONTENT CONSULTANT
CARLOS M. GRADIL, PhD
EXTENSION PROFESSOR
EQUINE STUDIES PROGRAM COORDINATOR
EQUINE REPRODUCTIVE SERVICES
UNIVERSITY OF MASSACHUSETTS AMHERST

Kids Core
An Imprint of Abdo Publishing
abdobooks.com

abdobooks.com

Published by Abdo Publishing, a division of ABDO, PO Box 398166, Minneapolis, Minnesota 55439. Copyright © 2022 by Abdo Consulting Group, Inc. International copyrights reserved in all countries. No part of this book may be reproduced in any form without written permission from the publisher. Kids Core™ is a trademark and logo of Abdo Publishing.

Printed in the United States of America, North Mankato, Minnesota.
102021
012022

THIS BOOK CONTAINS RECYCLED MATERIALS

Cover Photos: Alberto Menendez Cervero/Shutterstock Images, (mule); Simon Bratt/Shutterstock Images, (background)
Interior Photos: Olena Kurashova/Shutterstock Images, 4–5; Nikita Vishneveckiy/Shutterstock Images, 6; Evgeny Haritonov/Shutterstock Images, 9; Tracy Kerestesh/Shutterstock Images, 10, 16, 28 (bottom), 29 (bottom); Flaviano Fabrizi/Shutterstock Images, 12–13; Ihor Biliavskyi/Shutterstock Images, 15 (left), 15 (right); Lazyllama/Alamy, 19; Michel Seelen/Shutterstock Images, 20–21; Ezequiel Laprida/Shutterstock Images, 23; Shutterstock Images, 24, 29 (top); Dee Browning/Shutterstock Images, 25; Budimir Jevtic/Shutterstock Images, 26; Gonzalo de Miceu/Shutterstock Images, 28 (top)

Editor: Christine Ha
Series Designer: Katharine Hale

Library of Congress Control Number: 2021941171

Publisher's Cataloging-in-Publication Data

Names: Lilley, Matt, author.
Title: Stubborn as a mule: are mules headstrong? / by Matt Lilley
Other title: are mules headstrong?
Description: Minneapolis, Minnesota : Abdo Publishing, 2022 | Series: Animal idioms | Includes online resources and index.
Identifiers: ISBN 9781532196720 (lib. bdg.) | ISBN 9781644946510 (pbk.) | ISBN 9781098218539 (ebook)
Subjects: LCSH: Mules--Juvenile literature. | Donkeys--Behavior--Juvenile literature. | Obstinacy--Juvenile literature. | Animal instinct--Juvenile literature. | Idiomatic expressions--Juvenile literature.
Classification: DDC 636.183--dc23

CONTENTS

CHAPTER 1
A Stubborn Animal? 4

CHAPTER 2
Think Like a Mule 12

CHAPTER 3
Trust Your Mule 20

Mule Facts 28
Glossary 30
Online Resources 31
Learn More 31
Index 32
About the Author 32

Many animals can seem stubborn at times.

CHAPTER 1

A Stubborn Animal?

Alexandra was walking her dog, Hazel. Suddenly, Hazel stopped. Alexandra pulled on Hazel's leash. "Come on, Hazel. Let's go."

Hazel wouldn't budge. Alexandra pulled a little harder. But Hazel didn't move an inch. Alexandra got frustrated.

Sometimes when an animal is being stubborn, it may have reasons. It may be tired or scared.

Alexandra said, "Come on! Hazel, you are as stubborn as a mule!"

Hazel started pulling Alexandra back the other way. Then, Alexandra looked up and saw her friend Mason. He was waving and jogging toward them.

When he ran up to them, Hazel wagged her tail and greeted him. Alexandra looked at Hazel. Now she understood why Hazel didn't want to move!

"Is that why you wouldn't walk, Hazel? You saw Mason coming?" Hazel barked, and the three of them walked to the park together.

What Are Idioms?

Stubborn as a mule is an idiom. An idiom is an expression that is often used in a specific language. It usually means something other than the words that make up the idiom. *Stubborn as a mule* describes a person or animal that **refuses** to go along with what someone else says. A stubborn person or animal is usually being **unreasonable**.

Can Mules Have Babies?

Most mules are sterile. This means they cannot make babies. Female mules are called mollies. They can sometimes have babies, but it is very rare.

If trained, mules can be good guard animals. They will stomp and bite at threats.

People mix two types of animals hoping that the offspring will have the best features of both animals.

Alexandra compared Hazel to a mule because she thought Hazel was not listening to her and was being very stubborn.

A mule is a **hybrid** of two animals. A mule has a donkey for a father and a horse for a mother. Its **traits** are a mix of donkey and horse traits. For example, a mule has a horse-like body but donkey-like legs and ears. Are mules really stubborn? They may seem stubborn, but they know more than we may think!

Further Evidence

Visit the website below. Does it give any new evidence to support Chapter One?

Mule Facts

abdocorelibrary.com/stubborn-as-a-mule

Since mules are less likely to run from a dangerous situation than horses, they were used in the past to carry weapons and supplies during wars.

CHAPTER **2**

Think Like a Mule

Horses, donkeys, and mules are all prey animals. This means they are hunted for food by other animals. They survive by watching out for danger. When a horse senses danger, it tries to run first before fighting.

When facing danger, donkeys either freeze in place, attack, or run away. A donkey is more likely to try fighting to survive. Mules decide whether to fight or run.

Mule Senses

A mule uses all its senses to look for danger. With eyes on the sides of its head, a mule has a wide range of vision. It can also move its eyes in two different directions. When a mule sees something moving, it stays **alert** until it figures out that the moving object is not a threat.

Mules also have good hearing. Their ears are big and can rotate to listen better. Usually, their ears face the direction they are looking.

Blind Spots

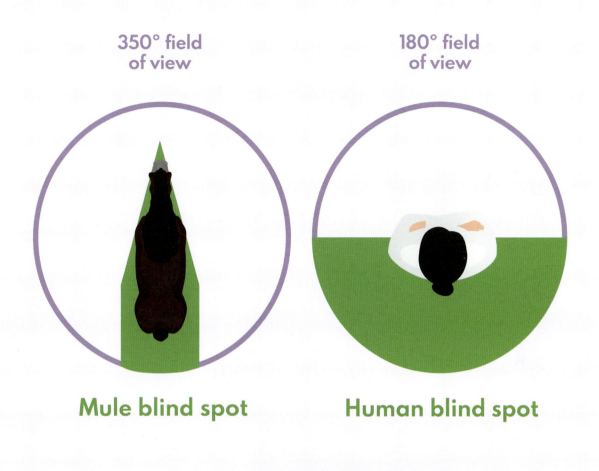

Mules can see 350 degrees around them. In comparison, humans can see for only about 180 degrees. But mules have blind spots in front and behind them. These are areas mules have trouble seeing. To make up for this, they can move their heads quickly to focus on things in their blind spots.

Mules can rotate their ears 180 degrees.

If a mule hears something, it tries to see what it is. Unfamiliar or loud noises make a mule nervous. It may want to run to safety.

Touch is another important sense for mules. A mule's skin is quite sensitive. A mule can feel a fly land on a single hair on its body. Things brushing against a mule's fur or whiskers might alert it to danger.

Tracking Two Things

Mules focus with their eyes and ears. The animals can focus one eye and ear on one thing and the other eye and ear on something else. This lets them track two things at once.

It can also feel vibrations through the ground with its hooves. This lets it know that something is coming. It can get ready to fight or flee if needed.

Mules are very good at sensing danger. Sometimes there isn't really any danger, but a mule needs to make sure it won't be hurt or attacked. At other times, a mule might be aware of danger that a human may not know about.

Explore Online

Visit the website below. Does it give any new information about mules?

Mules and Hinnies

abdocorelibrary.com/stubborn-as-a-mule

Though a mule's skin is sensitive, mules can still handle bad weather and strong sunlight better than horses.

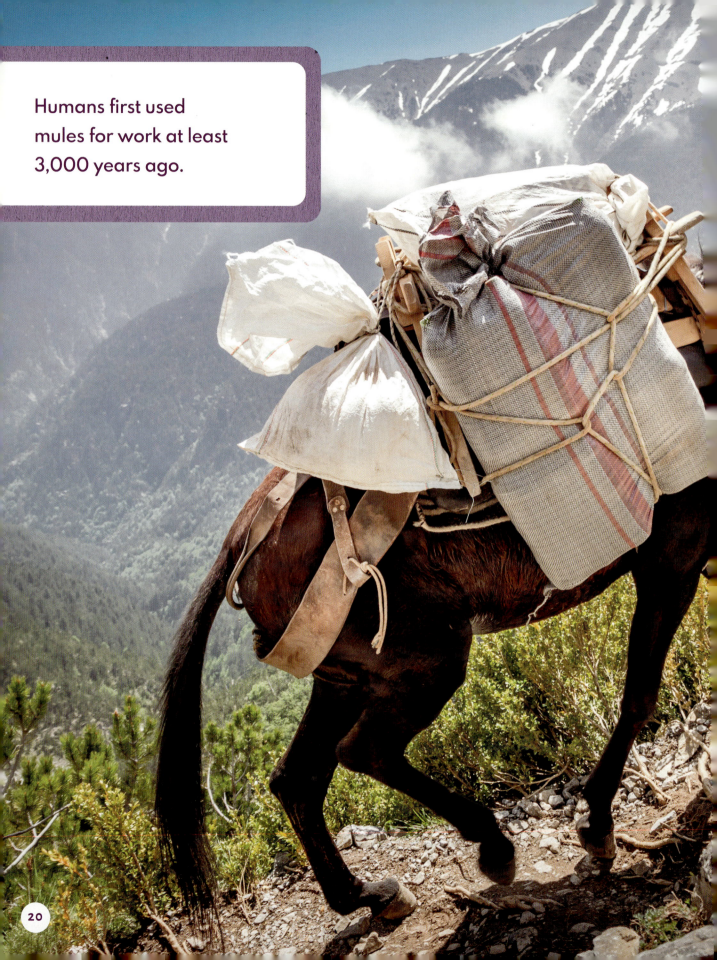

Humans first used mules for work at least 3,000 years ago.

Trust Your Mule

Mules help some humans with physical work. There are different types of mules for different types of work. For example, draft mules are big and strong. They can pull heavy loads. Pack mules have good feet and strong backs. They can carry lots of stuff. Saddle mules are used for riding.

Self-Preservation

While mules do the same jobs as horses and donkeys, they are considered smarter and more patient. Like horses, they make decisions on their own. But it is easier to make a horse work, even if the work is too much to handle. A mule will stop working if it thinks the task is unsafe or too difficult.

Mules Around the World

Mules have worked on every continent, including Antarctica. In 1912, the British Antarctic Expedition brought mules to the frozen continent to help pull supplies.

Mules' hooves are harder than horses' hooves. This means they travel better over rough and rocky paths.

Most mules can survive off cheap grains and grass. They also know not to overeat.

Mules are used around the world for transportation, farming, and carrying supplies.

Mules are good at **self-preservation**. Because of this, mules are less likely to get sick or hurt than horses. For example, a draft horse will try pulling a load that is too heavy for it. The horse might hurt itself trying to pull the load. A draft mule will not try to pull a load that is too big. The draft mule will refuse. A rider can force a horse to run farther than it can safely go. A saddle mule will stop if it gets too tired.

Mules are clever and quick to learn, making them good for training.

Is *stubborn as a mule* an accurate expression? Are mules really headstrong? The answer is no. When a mule refuses to cooperate, it might seem stubborn. But the mule is acting smart and protecting itself. Those who work with mules have a saying: "Trust your mule." These workers are aware that sometimes mules may know more than humans do!

Primary Source

Animal behaviorist Sue McDonnell explains mule behavior:

> Compared to horses, and even to donkeys, a mule's outward signs of fear, discomfort, or confusion are extremely muted. . . . It's easy for . . . [an] explosive escape or aggressive response to go unnoticed or to be misread as 'stubbornness.'

Source: Sue McDonnell. "Things to Remember When Working with Mules." *The Horse*, 22 Mar. 2018, www.thehorse.com. Accessed 29 June 2021.

What's the Big Idea?

Read this quote carefully. What is its main idea? Explain how the main idea is supported by details.

Mule Facts

Mules are strong and capable of doing hard work.

Mules have good senses that help them detect danger.

Mules are smarter than many people believe them to be. They can make their own decisions and are often aware of things humans may not know.

Mules are good at surviving. They know their limits and will not push themselves.

Glossary

alert
quick to notice danger or something out of place

hybrid
the offspring of two different types of plants or animals

refuse
to be unwilling to do something, often something someone else wants

self-preservation
the instinct to protect oneself from harm

traits
specific qualities, like physical features or behaviors

unreasonable
acting a certain, often negative, way without logical thinking

Online Resources

To learn more about mules, visit our free resource websites below.

Visit **abdocorelibrary.com** or scan this QR code for free Common Core resources for teachers and students, including vetted activities, multimedia, and booklinks, for deeper subject comprehension.

Visit **abdobooklinks.com** or scan this QR code for free additional online weblinks for further learning. These links are routinely monitored and updated to provide the most current information available.

Learn More

The Everything Book of Horses and Ponies. DK, 2019.

Thermes, Jennifer. *Horse Power: How Horses Changed the World.* Abrams, 2021.

Index

Antarctica, 22

blind spots, 15

donkeys, 11, 13–14, 22, 27
draft mules, 21, 25

hooves, 18
horses, 11, 13, 22, 25, 27
hybrid, 11

idioms, 7, 8, 26

mollies, 8

pack mules, 21
prey animals, 13

saddle mules, 21, 25
senses, 13, 14–18

About the Author

Matt Lilley is the author of more than a dozen books for children. He holds a Master's in scientific and technical writing from the University of Minnesota. He has also worked as an elementary school literacy tutor for Reading Corps, a division of AmeriCorps. He lives in Minnesota with his family.